For a thousand years
stories have been told in Prague,
magical, mysterious, romantic legends,
stories of love and adventure...

The book
Beautiful Stories of Golden Prague
that you hold in your hand
is an invitation to the world of ancient Prague stories.

Here you can read of old Bohemian rulers and artists, rich men of Prague and its poor, the renowned buildings of the ancient city, the loves of its people, their moments of happiness and of suffering. The fate of the Czech nation is reflected in the legends wreathing the capital city of the Bohemian kingdom. This selective choice of the most attractive Prague stories will be your guide on your walks through Prague.

This book will serve you
as a tourist guide
around the mystical world of Prague's legends.

Železný muž w platnýřské ulici

Beautiful Stories of Golden PRAGUE

Eduard Petiška, Jan M. Dolan

The Foundation of Prague, The Vyšehrad Treasures and the Golden Cradled, Bivoj the Strong, The Maidens' War, Horymír, Faust, Zuzana, The King and the Stars, Dalibor

by Eduard Petiška

The Devil's Pillar, The Foundation of Prague New Town, The Student Who Made Magic, The Fish, The Devil a Cook, The Church called Na Karlově, The Treasure of Poříčí, The Spring of St. Wenceslas, The Builder of the Charles Bridge, The Haughty Lady, About Master Hanuš, The Three Golden Roses, Rotlev, The Prague Red Indians, The Prisoner in the Little Quarter, The Hunger Wall, The Ball, Žito the Magician, The Church in Šárka, Prague Saint's Dedication Day, The Lamp

by Jan M. Dolan

ISBN: 80-901540-1-8

The Foundation of Prague

nce long ago a castle stood above the Vltava with wooden fortifications and a timbered palace within the fortifications. Later it was given the name Vyšehrad, meaning High Castle. It stood on the right bank of the river on a tall cliff, the feet of which were washed by restless waves. The castle was as firm as the will of the princes who ruled in it.

It is said that this is where Prince Přemysl used to sit on a stone princely throne and, together with Princess Libuše, received reports from all over his country, this is where he passed judgment and gave advice.

Under his rule the country changed ever more rapidly. The thick forests gave way to fields and among the fields hard-working hands built settlements and forts and strongholds. Prince Přemysl advised his people well. The more forts and castles there were in the land, the better the local people warded off the assaults of enemies. During the confusion of war they withdrew behind the mounds and ramparts, gathered supplies there and drove in their cattle too. Behind the ramparts they defended their lives and the lives of their families.

The tribe of the Czechs grew mightier and there was a need to find more and more homes. When asked where would be the most suitable place to found a new settlemet, Princess Libuše answered:

"Settle in a place where you will find four elements in good accord. Fertile, life-giving soil, pure water, healthy air and sufficient fuel for fire, where the trees afford both wood and shade. If harmony reigns among the elements, we shall want for nothing."

Then many families settled in the land according to Libuše's advice, and their fields yielded a rich harvest and their herds multiplied. A cheerful smoke rose to the skies from the fires of their new homes.

One day, when Prince Přemysl visited Princess Libuše's castle with her, they mounted with their retinue to the highest part of the castle. It was evening, and in the glow of the setting sun the landscape spread on all sides, bearing traces of human work. Fields alternated with settlements and pastures, the forest had retreated to the horizon and there kept guard like closed battle ranks. The dazzling sun dropped towards the forest and the shadow of the castle fell to the east. Princess Libuše turned to the moist blue shadows of advancing night, and suddenly everything of earth and in the atmosphere was seized by a great silence. None of the courtiers spoke, the wind held its breath and the birds, which had been singing till that moment, fell silent in the tree-tops. The princess stretched out her hand to the east and, as if in the cloudiness and evening mists she touched something in the distance, she moved her fingers gently and spoke:

"I see a great castle and its glory reaches to the stars. The place lies hidden in deep forests, from the north it is protected by the valley of the Brusnice stream, from the south by a wide rocky hill. The river Vltava makes its way beneath its slopes. Go there and in the midst of woods you will see a man chiselling the threshold of a house. Build a castle there and name it, according to the chiselled threshold, Praha.* And as even great men bow their heads as they cross a threshold, so will they bow them before this castle."

Prince Přemysl and the courtiers looked in that direction, but all they saw was the approaching night. The future was hidden in it like a precious stone in a hill.

For a further moment the princess pointed her white hand towards the distance, but then the spirit of prophesy withdrew

** Praha means threshold in Czech. Translator's note.*

and the sparkle in her eyes faded. And as is often the case with prophets and poets, when the enthusiasm languished in Libuše, it awoke in those who listened to her, and they started immediately to prepare for the journey.

With the dawn of the new day messengers set out for the east to find the place the princess had spoken of. They came upon the valley of a stream and a rocky hill, and they entered into woods from where regular blows could be heard. They found a man who was chiselling the threshold of a house.

They did not hesitate and buckled down to work. They felled trees, built long huts, raised ramparts. And so the castle Praha grew up on the left bank of the Vltava, wooden like Vyšehrad, but more spacious and more imposing in structure. The name Praha went from mouth to mouth throughout the land. And foreign merchants carried it to countries far away.

The Vyšehrad Treasures and the Golden Cradle

Princess Libuše gazed into the future, but she could also see into the bowels of the earth. It is said that her prophesies told which hill hid gold within it and which silver. That was the time as legend tells, when gold was discovered in Jílové and silver in Kutná Hora. And it is said that in those good old days there was such an abundance of silver and of gold that in places it sprouted from the ground like a shoot, needing only to be broken off. In those days a man was digging for gold near Jílové and he found such a lump of gold that it weighed more than the prince and princess. He sent that admirable and weighty piece of gold to Prince Přemysl at Vyšehrad. Přemysl consulted Princess Libuše and they summoned a sculptor who made the gold into a statue in the likeness of a man seated on a princely throne. They ordered that a special shelter should be built for the golden idol, and they went there to bow down to it and bring sacrifices in gratitude for the gifts that the Czechs enjoyed from their fertile and metal-rich land. They called the golden idol Zelú.

The gold and silver was laid into the underground halls of Vyšehrad, which are said to have been the treasury of the royal house ever since the days of Krok. And the cradle for Přemysl's and Libuše's son, Nezamysl, was also of gold.

The years passed by, and because they were happy years for the country and for the princely family, they passed quickly. The royal son Nezamysl was already trying to draw a bow and to lift his father's sword. Libuše felt pride in her son, and her heart also felt sorrow over passing time, that rules even rulers. She told her maidens to take the golden cradle and follow her. The princess stopped at a place below Vyšehrad where the river had milled out such a depth that the surface was darker there.

NEZAMYSL
MNATA
WO
IEN
1905.

"Let the cradle down into the depths," she ordered the maidens.

The heavy golden cradle sank in the water, there was just a brief flash and it disappeared. But the princess watched it fixedly and she saw its long fall through waters and through centuries. And she saw light in the depths of the ages, and at one time it was the glow of the sun, at another a fire, and she heard noise and shouting, and at one time it was cheering and singing, at another cries and weeping. The golden cradle floated down deeper and deeper among the waters of tears.

"Hide yourself, hide!" called the princess, "and one day, cleansed by the tears of those who live in this land, you will emerge from the waves and good hands will grasp you and will lay in you a child who will bring salvation to the country and its people."

The princess fell silent and returned to Vyšehrad.

And the cradle was like a golden grain, sown to germinate one day. And the secret Vyšehrad treasure was like a precious grain too, that would provide bread for all the hungry when the need in the land was greatest. But the most precious grain sown in the future was the youngest generation, of which Nezamysl was one.

And then, many centuries later, when a son, Wenceslas, was born to Queen Eliška, a strange thing came about. The waters of the Vltava opened like the flower of a rose and gave out their ancient treasure from the depths. The golden cradle that Princess Libuše had once entrusted to the river below the Vyšehrad cliff. And it was the cradle in which, according to the prophesy, only he might be fostered who would bring our land peace and happiness. Now it left the bed of the Vltava and offered its golden embrace to little Wenceslas, son of John of Luxenburg.

He whom the cradle took into itself, the young Prince Wenceslas, became the greatest sovereign of the Czech nation and entered history under the name of Charles IV., Father of his Country.

When Charles IV. breathed his last, it is said that at that very moment the golden bed that had stood in Karlštejn Castle during the emperor's lifetime, disappeared. It turned into a cradle and the golden cradle returned to the Vltava below the Vyšehrad cliff.

Sometimes a golden ray is released from the cradle, it rises from the depths and touches the undulating surface of the river. Perhaps it is surveying whether the right moment has not come.

It is said that one day the golden cradle will again leave the Vltava and a mother will lay a new-born babe into the cradle who will bring the country peace and happiness. But who knows? Perhaps the cradle already stands somewhere in Bohemia, and perhaps there is not only one.

Bivoj the Strong

ne day Libuše was riding to the castle over the Vltava that was later named Vyšehrad. She was accompanied not only by her train of maidens but by her elder sister Kazi. Kazi liked to journey to these parts. She was enticed there by a memory. Several times on the way to the castle she had caught sight of a man on whom her eyes lighted with pleasure. That man lived in a settlement not far away.

Towards evening the sisters reached the castle. When they dismounted from their horses the long shadows of the timbered buildings were flowing together on the ground, and the sun was seting after its day-long pilgrimage only on the roofs and tips of the battlements. Libuše and Kazi climbed to a height behind the castle rampart and gazed down towards the sparkling Vltava. The forested slopes of Petřín breathed a scent across the river as strong as rare spices.

Then from the other end of the courtyard came the sound of many excited voices shouting. Libuše and Kazi looked back and saw a crowd of men. In their midst walked a stalwart young man. Bending forward he bore some burden on his back. Kazi recognized that young man as the one she had seen on her visits to the castle.

The young man advanced to before the two sisters and the crowd formed a semicircle round them. All looked at his burden in admiration. A huge, live wild boar that he had overcome with his bare hands in the marshy forest down by the river. He carried it with its bristly back pressed to his own back, holding it by its hairy ears. The boar blinked its blood-shot eyes furiously and spattered its capturer's hempen shirt with saliva.

"Bivoj, Bivoj!" the shouts rose again in the crowd and the name resounded as praise of that unprecedented deed, in admiration and gratitude. The enormous boar that the man had brought to the castle had been wreaking harm on the villagers' fields for many weeks and it had seemed to be invulnerable. How many arrows they had let fly at him from their bows, how many spears hurled at him, but the wild beast had shaken off death as a bird shakes off feathers.

Now it was to die before Libuše, the ruler of her people, as if at her decision.

Pride sparkled in Libuše's eyes that such a brave and strong man lived in the tribe of the Czechs. But her sister Kazi's eyes glowed with enthusiasm and favour.

Bivoj threw his burden off his back and, as the boar rushed at him he pierced it with his spear, not retreating so much as an inch.

The courtyard buzzed with praise.

The young victor stood there, dewed with sweat, firmly grasping a short sword, determined to put an end to the harmful boar, should it gather strength for another attack. But his precise blow with the spear had been fatal.

"Bivoj, Bivoj!" The courtyard rang with joyful cries.

Such a deed deserved praise and a reward.

Libuše gave orders that a feast should be given in the hero's honour, and she and her sister Kazi went to choose a gift for the victor from their father Krok's treasury - a belt decorated with golden discs. Then Kazi herself girded Bivoj with it.

And night fell and fires flared and over them pieces of boar's meat were roasted. The bitter mead awoke the memories of old warriors. They related who had behaved as a hero and when, who had strong arms, a sure eye and good luck. Hunts long ago and past battles and old tales flew round the light of the fire like night butterflies.

Apart from the joyful feast, where the flames' light only reached when more wood was put on the fire, apart from the loud talk, Kazi and Bivoj stood quietly conversing together. Only the glitter of a gold belt from the darkness betrayed that Bivoj had not gone. And he was not to go alone.

At dawn next day Kazi said farewell to her sister Libuše and left the castle on the steep cliff over the Vltava. She was making for her own castle Kazín and Bivoj rode beside her.

The Maidens' War

Old legends tell of the ancient rights of women. Women chose their husbands and the husbands lived in their wives' family.

When Princess Libuše, who defended the rights of women, died, the women lost their advocate. Prince Přemysl was on the side of the men. Theirs was the power and the right to rule. And just as once a man had mocked women before Libuše's court, saying they had long hair but were short on brains, so now a woman rose amongst the people and ridiculed the bearded mens' chins dripping with mead. The name of that young woman was Vlasta. She had been in Princess Libuše's escort and she bore hard the changes that spread from Vyšehrad and the forts to the villages and lonely farmsteads.

Vlasta gathered girls and young women around her. They all liked her words and none of those who followed her wanted to submit to the mastery of men.

On the left bank of the Vltava, opposite Vyšehrad, rose a long-topped hill. Vlasta took her maidens there and called on them to build a castle. The girls agreed enthusiastically and they did build a strong castle. They lived there as men live in castles, they practised shooting with the bow and rode out hunting in the Vltava forests. Prince Přemysl looked out perturbed from the heights of Vyšehrad at the new maidens' castle on the opposite bank of the river. He had a council called of the leading men of the tribe and he said to them:

"You certainly know of the new castle that the girls have built and that they call Děvín. This night I had an evil dream. Because of this bad dream and the unhappy castle I have summoned you. Listen to what I dreamed. I thought I saw a young maid who charged through our land as if crazed, with flying hair and contorted face. The streams ran with blood instead of water and the maid, like a rabid wolf, drank of this blood. Then she ran up to me and offered me too a bowl of blood."

The men listened to Přemysl's speech and they smiled. Děvín, they thought to themselves, is but a girl's game, and after a time every game tires. What sort of warriors could women ever be? And they ignored Přemysl's warning and listened only to their own conceit.

In the meantime Vlasta prepared the girls in Děvín for battle with the men. She divided the garrison of girls into three parts. She chose from the wisest and most courageous counsellors and guards, who stood guard over the castle. She taught the most beautiful girls flattering speeches and beguiling ways with men. They then lured men with sweet words and pleasant looks, just as huntsmen lure game with decoys. Woe to the man who fell into the clutches of such a beauty. He was annihilated. The third group of girls trained in using arms.

One of the worst things was that not a single man lived in Děvín, though in Vyšehrad and other castles and in the villages plenty of women still lived who were Vlasta's spies and who procured both weapons and horses for Děvín. So it happened that the men had neither enough weapons nor enough horses, and Vlasta and her counsellors knew their every movement, but the men had no news of the strength of the girls.

"It will be enough for us to advance on Děvín," said the men, "it will be enough for them just to see from Děvín a column of warriors, and they will take fright and open the gates to us."

In vain did Prince Přemysl warn them, he counselled them in vain.

The men assembled, each of them grabbed some weapon, but none of them believed that he would use a weapon. They advanced towards the maidens' castle without Přemysl and in cheerful mood. They were relying on feminine fear. The men climbed the hill towards the maidens' castle, and it seemed as if life had died out in Děvín. There was not a movement anywhere.

"You see?" the men called to one another, "no sooner do we show ourselves, and they hide from us like mice."

They went forward, not knowing they were watched from the castle by as many eyes as there were arrow slits in the ramparts. When they approached within shooting distance, the gates of Děvín flew open and girls on horseback with spears rushed out amongst the amazed men, headed by Vlasta, their commander. She herself pierced seven of the best men with her spear who, stunned with astonishment, never even raised their swords. The archeresses, whom the men had laughed at till then, sent a cloud of arrows over the confused warriors. The men's ranks wavered, some fell, others limped to the nearby forest, some still tried to encourage one another, but in vain. Vlasta and her maiden warriors held the field.

Sadly did the men return to Vyšehrad. Too late they recognized that Přemysl had spoken wisely. Tidings of the men's defeat spread round the country. All women held up their heads proudly. The thought of Děvín gave them strength. Some were indeed proud, but for love of their men did not leave them. Some were blinded by pride and they fled to Děvín. But to some pride gave new eyes, and the husbands of those women went out into the woods at night. They were afraid to sleep at their wives' sides, lest their lives should be taken from them in sleep.

The maidens' army grew from day to day. Armed gangs of girls rode through the land, and wherever they heard that a woman was still living in harmony with her husband, they shattered their content with cunning or with arms.

Slowly and with difficulty the men began to arm and to get horses. This time Prince Přemysl would not allow the fight to begin till the men were properly armed. Until then they were to be cautious and not believe even the most flattering girlish words. Yet always someone was to be found who did believe honeyed words from maidens' mouths and doubted the prince's good advice.

At that time Prince Přemysl sent one of his men, Ctirad, to settle a dispute between two clans, who had settled in a distant place on the left river bank. The whole of Vyšehrad knew of Ctirad's journey, and what Vyšehrad knew soon came to be known in Děvín. And at once there were girls who were ready to prepare a trap for Ctirad. They chose the most beautiful amongst them, Šárka, and went with her to the forest till they reached the path that Ctirad must take with his company. Here by the wayside they sat the lovely Šárka on an up-rooted tree trunk and bound her so firmly with straps that they bit into her skin. And so bitter was Šárka's hatred of men that she felt no pain, only delight at the trap being sprung. When the girls had bound Šárka, they laid a jug of mead beside her, hung a hunting horn on her neck and left her there. They hid in the forest not far away, together with their horses, and waited for their moment.

Šárka started weeping and wailing till the tree-covered valley echoed with her cries and multiplied them till the frightened birds deserted their nests.

Ctirad and his men heard her lament from afar and spurred on their horses. When they were near the place from whence the cries came, a raven circled over them and cawed as in foreboding. But the men had no notion that the ominous cawing was addressed to them. They watched the raven as it disappeared behind the tree-tops, and when they looked down to the ground they saw the up-rooted tree with an extremely beautiful girl tied to it.

"Help me, good people, help," called Šárka weeping, and the men believed her tears and moans.

They all jumped from their horses and Ctirad himself cut through her bonds. Šárka fell at Ctirad's feet and pretended gratitude. Ctirad was touched and, lifting her to her feet, asked her what had happened and who had bound her.

"Oh Sir," said Šárka, "I was out hunting with my father and his train, and when I was chasing a doe I became separated from the others and I got lost. At last I came out of the wood onto this path, and I took it joyfully, because I heard horses neighing ahead of me. I thought they were the horses of my father's company. But I was wrong. I came upon a bunch of girls from Děvín. Those cruel creatures took me prisoner and bound me till the straps bit into my skin. They mocked me for not having gone with them to Děvín earlier, for staying with my old father. When I wept, they laughed all the more. Perhaps the heat and the mead they had drunk had gone to their heads. But as soon as they heard the clatter of horses' hoofs, they were afraid it was my father and his men returning. They left me bound here and hastily mounted their horses. Look, in their haste they even forgot their jug of mead."

"Fancy," Ctirad and his people were surprised, "mead from the maidens' castle. I wonder what it tastes like?"

Ctirad tried the mead, and his men did too, and they liked it. It was not any ordinary mead. Vlasta, the maidens' commander, had bewitched it. Whoever drank of it once became drowsy, he who drank twice could not hold his sword, and he who drank of it three times fell to the ground, overcome with sleep.

The men of Ctirad's retinue did not restrain themselves and they drank once, they drank twice and three times, and lay down in the forest grass that was silky as a maiden's tresses. They fell asleep and dreamt of victory over Děvín.

Ctirad drank twice and felt himself to be weak and torpid. Šárka took the horn from her neck and said with a smile:

"Sir, I am too weak after what I have suffered. But perhaps you could blow this horn. If my father is somewhere in the forest with his company, he will hurry here as soon as he hears the sound of this well-known horn."

Ctirad grasped the horn and blew it with the last of his strength. That was the sign the girls hidden in the thickets were waiting for. They leapt on their horses, rode like the wind, and surrounded Ctirad, Šárka and the sleeping men. The enchanted drink had taken Ctirad's strength. He soon gave in. The girls bound him and Šárka, whose bonds he had so lately cut, helped them to do it. The girls killed Ctirad's company on the spot. Not a man was able to raise himself from the grass and all of them went from sleep straight into death. Then the girls led Ctirad to Děvín between their horses like a slave who had escaped his master. The scene of this deceit and betrayal is still called Šárka today and it is said that for a long time the laughter and howling of evil spirits could be heard there, delighting over human perfidy.

The fighting girls erected a wheel in front of Děvín, into which they entwined the tortured Ctirad. The men of Vyšehrad saw their cruel work and counted the days that separated them from the moment of revenge. The time was ripening, the numbers of spears, swords, shields, bows and arrows grew like spring wheat. Evil begat weapons and weapons were preparing to beget evil.

Vlasta knew of the arming at Vyšehrad, but she was so sure of her power that she merely smiled at the men's doings. However Ctirad's death had armed the men better than smiths and armourers.

They did not even wait for the day of revenge, which was to be decided by Prince Přemysl, but grief and anger over Ctirad's slaying drove them into the forests, where they attacked bands of the Děvín amazons and slaughtered them without mercy.

As soon as news of this was brought to Vlasta she was seized by such fury as a she-bear that has lost her cubs. She rushed into the Děvín courtyard and ordered an assault on Vyšehrad that would rock it to its foundations.

The men saw the approaching army of women from the battlements and rode out to meet it. Both sides spurred their horses, both sides were spoiling for the fight.

A terrible battle broke out, such as had never been seen or heard of, for a father was opposed by his daughter, a brother by his sister and a husband by his wife. The struggle knew no mercy, anyone who hesitated, if only for a moment, paid for their delay with their lives. The most reckless of all was Vlasta. She darted forward on her horse, without a glance to right or left, as if she wanted to reach the gates of Vyšehrad and destroy the castle single-handed. Not one of the maidens could keep up with her. Too late Vlasta realized that she had got too far from her band. Seven young men surrounded her, closed in upon her, and seven knives ended her life.

Confusion reigned in the band of girls. Many of them turned their horses back to Děvín, but the men followed them right into the castle courtyard.

There fell Vlasta's counsellors, and there too fell the beauties who had lured men into snares with cunning, even the skilful archeresses fell. The earth was soaked with blood as it is with rain in the days of autumn. Šárka too perished in the Děvín courtyard, at the hand of Ctirad's son.

Prince Přemysl decreed that the maidens' castle should be set on fire and destroyed. The castle died with its amazons.

Děvín burned long into the night and the conflagration could be seen over the whole land. Now even sceptics could see that those who help themselves to victory through treachery unerringly prepare their own defeat.

Horymír

During the reign of Prince Křesomysl there stood between Beroun and Příbram, below the rolling slopes of Housina, the fortress of Neumětely. It stood in meadows, protected by bulwarks and ramparts, that enclosed it as a ring encloses a finger. In front of the ramparts was a deep moat, and the water that was let into the moat prevented intruders from approaching the ramparts. The thane Horymír lived in this fortress and presided over the surrounding land. So legend relates.

During the years of Křesomysl's rule a longing for gold and silver spread immensely amongst the people. Many of them left their villages and made their way to the gold-bearing rivers in the south of our country. Many a ploughman exchanged his plough for a pan in which he washed river sand, instead of sowing grain for bread he picked grains of gold from the sand. Others went to places indicated by ancient prophesy and opened up the earth and broke the rocks, to take precious metal from the heart of the land. Life shifted from the fields and hamlets to the banks of rivers and to hills and mountains. The forest sent wild weeds and brushwood into the orphaned fields and the deserted hamlets. It reclaimed soil that man had previously taken from it.

And there were many who feared for the state of the land. They came to Prince Křesomysl in Vyšehrad and called for the situation to be righted. Horymír of Neumětely was one of those who came before the prince.

"Take note, Prince," he complained, "our fields are ploughed by wild boar, our fields are sown with the seeds of the forest and rocky hillsides, our fields are harvested by the wind. Where are we to get bread, if everyone goes away to search for metal? We shall waste away with hunger and starvation will also afflict those who have set out for the rivers and the mountains. Give orders, Prince, that the people should keep to the old customs and return to their fields and their flocks."

Prince Křesomysl assented to Horymír's words and promised that he would put things to rights. But scarcely had Horymír left for the Neumětely fortress, than the prince's mind inclined in the other direction. Křesomysl found it pleasant to accept precious metals from the gold-diggers and to swell the princely treasure with both taxes and gifts. Greed for the wealth that was hidden in the earth had seized him too.

If I take the side of Horymír, the side of the dissatisfied thanes, I shall gain nothing for myself, the prince reflected, but if I take the side of the gold-diggers my Vyšehrad treasure will increase.

And because he had enough bread himself, the hunger of others did not weigh upon him.

The thanes waited in vain for the promised righting of affairs, Horymír waited in vain for the prince's favour. It seemed that the old customs were irretrievably lost.

But the news of Horymír's complaint spread amongst the gold-diggers. It was passed from quarry to quarry, from pit to pit, and hatred of Horymír flared up sharply, for not one of the gold-diggers wanted to leave his new craft.

"The best thing would be to kill Horymír," advised the hottest heads.

"We'll stuff bread down his gullet till it suffocates him," cried others.

And the ones joined with the others and they set out for Horymír's fortress. Their motive was revenge.

Horymír saw from afar the rampageous people approaching, armed with hoes, crowbars and clubs. He could not stand up to such a multitude. So he went to find his best friend. His best friend was not a man, but the faithful horse Šemík. Šemík turned his big, wise eyes on Horymír and he read in his face that disaster was upon them. Horymír stroked the horse, swung onto his back and called:

"Rise up, Šemík!"

Šemík reared up and leapt with Horymír across the ramparts and the moat and disappeared into the forest.

Then the gold-diggers overran Horymír's estate like locusts, destroying and plundering, they scattered the stacks, took the corn and in the end they resorted to fire. That completed the destruction of Horymír's estates.

Then the gold-diggers wound their way from Neumětely to their work, in high spirits at their easy victory, and on the way they jeered:

"Horymír need not fear hunger any more. Now he will just be hungry."

But violence never comes singly. It calls for further violence. When Horymír came home in the evening and found nothing but ashes and smouldering beams, he swore by the first star over the horizon and by all the mysterious beings of the waters, the meadows and the forests that the gold-diggers should pay for that injustice.

He leapt up on Šemík and rushed through the forest and the darkness to the gold-diggers' mines. On the way he called the spirits of the night to his aid, and the spirits flew down to him and rushed forward with him.

Wherever the seekers after metal had opened the earth, Horymír closed it again. The night spirits helped him to sweep stones, clay and sand into the holes and pits. They helped him to set fire to the gold-diggers' huts and cabins and raced hotfoot on their way.

But in the morning Horymír stood among the prince's courtiers in Vyšehrad as fresh as if he had slept all night.

Soon a long procession of gold-diggers came to Vyšehrad, they shook their fists in the direction of Horymír.

"Is it true what these men say?" Křesomysl asked Horymír. "And if it is true, why do you harm them? He who harms them harms me."

"Is it not beyond the power of a single man to do so much work in a single night?" Horymír replied. He did not say whether what the gold-diggers spoke was the truth, nor did he say it was lies.

But the gold-diggers knew of no other culprit. It was Horymír whom they had most harmed, and so they were convinced that he too had harmed them most.

When the prince realised how long it would take before the gold-diggers could undo the damage and before the earth would again yield up its treasure, when he realised the greatness of his loss, he fell into a great fury. He commanded that Horymír, ravager of the prince's treasury, should be imprisoned and guarded until such time as sentence should be passed on him.

Křesomysl called a council of elders, but his anger shortened the consultation. The sentence was: Horymír shall pay for his deeds with his own head. And because many of the gold-diggers asserted that they had recognized Horymír as he galloped towards them in the light of the flames with drawn sword, the prince declared that Horymír should die by his own sword.

The gold-diggers in the Vyšehrad courtyard burst into cheers. Horymír bowed his head, but at once raised it again.

"Prince," he said, "if I must indeed depart this life, grant me one wish, that I may for the last time take a ride on my horse."

Křesomysl nodded that the condemned man's last wish should be fulfilled. But he ordered that the castle gates should be shut. Servants brought Šemík to Horymír, Horymír whispered something to him and leapt up onto him. As soon as he was in the saddle he shouted and the horse spun round beneath him.

He shouted a second time and Šemík took off and made a great leap from the gates to the ramparts. Křesomysl and the whole gathering were amazed. Horymír shouted for the third time and called:

"Rise up, Šemík!"

Those who stood nearby said that they heard Šemík answer in a human voice:

"Hold on, Master."

And like an arrow leaving the string of a bow, the horse and rider rose into the air, passing over the ramparts and the hollows below the cliff, over the shining surface of the Vltava, landing on the opposite bank of the river. It is said that the tracks of his hoofs were long to be seen in the stone.

In Vyšehrad everyone ran to the ramparts and they saw that both horse and rider were alive and sound and that they were making for home, for Neumětely. The prince was dumbfounded, as were the elders and the people.

Prince Křesomysl was brought to relent by the persuasion of the councillors and by his own fear. For who could survive such a leap but one who is protected by the gods? He sent messengers to the Neumětely fortress to announce to Horymír that he was forgiven.

Horymír outlived the gold-diggers' hatred, the prince's anger and the great leap, but his horse had injured himself by that leap. From that day he began to waste away.

"My dear Master," Šemík addressed Horymír one day, "my strength is rapidly failing, and soon we shall have to part. I fulfilled your wish, now you can fulfil mine. Do not let the crows and ravens nor the wolves scatter me about the land, but bury me before the gates of your court. So shall I be with you even after death."

Horymír fulfilled his Šemík's wish and for centuries the whole country has told of their faithful friendship.

The Devil's Pillar

nce long ago, during a cruel winter, a poor man from a Prague suburb went out into the woods to gather a little firewood.

He was afraid of his return home - he would go back with the wood, the wife and children would warm themselves, but he did not know where to get the money so that they could eat on the morrow. And in addition, his wife was expecting a child...

He was walking through the forest deep in black thoughts when he heard a voice behind him. He turned round and saw a huntsman.

The poor man complained to the huntsman of his fate.

"I'll help you," said the huntsman. "You will grow rich and all you do will succeed. You don't believe me? You will see. I want but one thing: you will give me what your wife is holding in her hand when you return."

Quickly the huntsman took out a bond.

The poor man did not hesitate, he signed - in his own blood - as the huntsman wished.

He took his bundle of wood and hurried home. It never occurred to him that the huntsman was the devil. He thought he was some kind of good wizard.

On entering the door he stood rigid.

His wife came to welcome him and in her arms she held the new-born child.

From that day on the poor man had no peace.

He lived very well, he grew rich, everything he touched brought him gain.

But he kept remembering his meeting with the huntsman.

He knew now that it was the devil. Straight after his return from the forest he confided his cares to a wise neighbour, and he advised him to have the child christened Peter, and then surely St. Peter would come to his aid. The unhappy father did so, but he still did not believe that he had saved his child from hell. When St. Peter appeared to him in a dream and assured him that he would not desert his son, he was a little calmer - but his guilt dogged his footsteps. To help his son as much as he could, he decided that he should become a priest. After all, the devil wouldn't carry off a priest, he said, and he looked forward to his son's first mass, which he was to serve in the Vyšehrad church. Now the devil will no longer have any right to him, he thought, and was pleased at how he had got the better of the devil.

But in the morning before mass the devil came for his soul.

St. Peter was keeping guard over his namesake - he said that if the devil wanted to carry off the priest's soul, he would give him one condition.

He must fly to Rome, to the church of St. Peter, take one pillar there, tear it out and bring it to Vyšehrad before the young priest had finished serving his first mass in the church.

The devil agreed.

He flew straight to Rome, flew over the Alps and descended on the Eternal City - but instead of taking a pillar from the church of St. Peter he took one from the church of Our Lady Travestere, which was nearer - and was pleased at how he had got the better of St. Peter by shortening his way to Bohemia. He flew back quickly with the pillar on his shoulder. But St. Peter helped his ward again. He caught hold of the devil and dragged him down into the lagoon in Venice. The pillar fell to the bottom, and before he brought it up the devil had really been delayed a lot. He cursed and hurried on as quickly as he could. St. Peter caught hold of him again, and again the pillar sunk to the bed of the lagoon. That was how St. Peter delayed the devil and in the meantime the priest was serving mass in Vyšehrad - his father, in the clutches of terror, sat on the

1904.

bench in front of him and waited till the devil's wings rustled over Vyšehrad.

The devil was tearing across the sky with the pillar over his shoulder, now it really looked as though the priest would not finish his first mass in time...

But the priest had just spoken the last word when the devil flew in. It would have been enough for him to be later by a single second, and he would have fallen through to hell - so the devil had to admit that he had lost to St. Peter. In a fury he lifted the pillar above his head and smashed it down on the Vyšehrad church. The pillar crashed through the roof and fell in front of the altar. In falling it was broken into three pieces. But his fury did not help the devil. The young priest was saved and a great weight fell from the mind of his old father, much greater than the weight of the Roman pillar... For a long time people pointed to the broken pillar in the church and remembered the good St. Peter, who had saved the young man. Then they took the pillar out of the church, and the Roman pillar ended up in the Vyšehrad garden. There too people went to look at it for many years.

The three parts of the broken pillar were a warning to all who might want to sell themselves to the devil...

The Foundation of Prague New Town

Once of an evening the Bohemian king and Roman emperor of the House of Přemyslides, Charles IV. sat by the window of Prague Castle and he and all his company gazed at the city, lovely in the light of early evening. Snow had touched the roofs with silver and the blanched beauty of the town was borne up to the castle windows.

The Bohemian king looked with delight at the capital city of his kingdom, prophesying it glory, as the Princess Libuše, his ancestress, had done. Then he invited the astrologer to speak too about the future of Prague.

The astrologer remained a moment in melancholy silence and then he spoke.

"If you command me to speak, my king, I will tell you what I know - but rather would I offer you - reconsider your request..."

The king repeated it.

"The fate of this city is written in the stars above our heads. In them, as in silver letters, its whole future is written and this sparkling inscription, my king, bodes no good... Behold, the town below the castle, the Little Quarter, will be consumed by fire, look across the river to the Old Town - it will be destroyed by floods. The whole of Prague - so it is written in the stars, will perish..."

The Bohemian king was silent for a while, reflecting.

Then he looked round at his frightened listeners and said: "You are wrong, astrologer. My beloved Prague will not perish. Perhaps what you say you read in silver letters on the sky will come about. But I shall found a New Town of Prague, I shall found it above the Old Town of Prague - and that town, you shall know, will not perish!"

And straightway he told his guests what the New Town that he would found would look like, where it would start and how far it would reach, where its gates would be - and his guests were amazed at the magnificence and magnanimity of the town that the king had dreamt up.

Faust

an has always longed for his wishes to be fulfilled. But each man goes after the fulfilment of his wishes in a different way.

In the old days, before the existence of Prague New Town, a house stood on the hillside that sloped down to the Vltava. When the New Town grew up during the reign of Charles IV. the buildings of the great new square, where later cattle markets were held, took this house amongst them. The house did not change its place, but in the course of centuries it changed its face.

It was said not to be a happy site on which the house was built. It stood near an ancient heathen place of sacrifice and was for ever caught in a net of mysterious superstitions. There were underground passages leading from the house, one as far as the Town Hall of the New Town, and these further multiplied the mystery of the house. And its inhabitants? Learned men had lived there, doctors, alchemists and people who dealt in strange sciences. During the rule of Emperor Rudolph II. the English alchemist Kelley lived in this house, and he was not the last of a long line of alchemists and scholars.

It is said that at one time the learned Doctor Faust also lived in the old house at the corner of the square. Legend gives us back his face, his figure and his deeds from the depths of time.

He is bending over retorts and glass jars in his alchemist's laboratory, watching a bubbling mixture in a cauldron and stroking his long dark beard thoughtfully. He goes up to a stand on which is a great thick book, where secret signs are written instead of letters. Faust's face in the candlelight is very pale and in that paleness only his eyes burn with an eager flame.

What was it Faust longed for? The fulfilment of his wishes? But the less his learning fulfilled them, the greater and more difficult to fulfil those wishes became. When he no longer knew where to turn, it is said he sought help from the devil. He reached for a thick book in which were written seven times seven ways in which to invoke the forces of hell. Faust made a mighty spell and the devil emerged from a cloud of smoke. He had a contract already prepared for Faust.

"Just sign it," said the devil, "and I will serve you for seven years and fulfil your every wish. But after seven years you will be mine, body and soul."

Seven years of wishes fulfilled, thought Faust, what wonderful luck has come my way. People live even ten times seven years, and how many of their wishes are granted? Seven years of wishes fulfilled equals thousands of years. In those seven years I shall come to know all the secrets and all the delights of this world. Faust took up a quill, the devil scratched his finger with a claw, and Faust signed the contract with his own blood.

From that moment on it is said there was nothing the devil denied Faust. Overnight Faust became a rich man. The chest in which he had been used to keep a small pouch of money, overflowed with silver and gold. And whenever Faust took a handful of coins from it, the gold and silver at once filled the space in the chest. Faust did not sow but he did reap, and he never reaped all.

What Faust could buy for money in seven years he bought, what he could not buy the devil got for him.

In those old times clumsy carts and unwieldy carriages jolted along bad roads. Travelling caused people many hardships. Stones and potholes ambushed the ways, and where the route lay through a forest it was dangerous to journey. Who knew in what thicket highwaymen were waiting for the carriage? Only Faust travelled comfortably in those times, safely and speedily. In Erfurt, in the German land, Faust had

a friend. This friend was very devoted to Faust and used sometimes to visit him in Prague. One day Faust sat down alone to supper in Prague, and in Erfurt his friend also sat down to table. But not alone. He had invited a party of friends. And as they supped and drank in Erfurt the company grew merry. The host thought of Faust:

"Ah, if he were only with us, then we should indeed be merry!"

Then a young man got up, raised his goblet and called:

"Faust, Faust, I drink to you, do you hear me? Where are you, that you are not with us? Can your Prague house be dearer to you than the company of friends?"

At that moment someone knocked at the gate. A servant ran to open it and Faust rode into the porch on horseback.

The terrified servant ran to his master in the banqueting hall.

"Sir, oh Sir, Doctor Faust has just arrived, he has dismounted from his horse and is coming up the stairs behind me."

The host thought at first that the servant was drunk. But before he could answer Faust stood in the doorway.

"Good evening, gentlemen," he said, "you called me and so here I am."

It took a while for the host and his friends to recover from their surprise. But Faust behaved so naturally and casually that they soon felt at ease. They received him amongst them and Faust was full of jokes and the company full of laughter.

"How is it, Master Faust," asked the young man who had summoned Faust with his toast, "that you were able to be at one moment in Prague and the next with us here in Erfurt?"

"I have an unusual horse," Faust explained, "but I cannot stay with you till morning. I must be back in Prague before dawn."

All those around the table were astounded. Faust wanted to make the return jouney that same night!

"Sir," the host's servant ran in again, "that horse," he complained, "that horse... I cannot give him enough oats. I give him oats, but as soon as I turn round they are gone. Ten horses would not get through as much oats as he does."

"Just don't feed him," said Faust, "that horse will devour whatever you put before him. He has had enough. The horse has had his oats and we shall treat ourselves to wine," Faust turned to the guests. "What kind would you like? Rhine wine, or wine from Spain, France, Bohemia or Hungary?"

The host and his friends laughed and shouted:

"Best would be all of them."

"As you wish," Faust nodded and asked for a gimlet. With the gimlet he drilled a hole in the side of the table and stopped up the hole with a cork. Five times he drilled the wood and five times he corked the holes. Then he asked for a goblet. He held it to the first hole, took out the cork and wonder of wonders, Rhine wine gushed from the opening. He held another goblet under the second opening and look, from that second hole springs the sweet red wine of Spain, from the third streams a golden current of French wine, from the fourth hole spouts red wine from Mělník and from the fifth dark fiery Hungarian wine.

Each of the guests could choose according to his taste and there was no end to the merriment. At midnight the horse neighed in the stable. The neighing went through the walls as if the horse were standing at the festive board.

"I must go," said Faust and got up to leave. But his friend detained him.

An hour later the neighing could be heard again. Again Faust stood up and again they detained him.

When the horse neighed for the third time, till the windows rattled, Faust would not allow himself to be delayed by anyone or anything.

They accompanied him before the gates of the house. Faust mounted the horse and the horse broke into a gallop. At first it kept to the cobblestones. Then the whole company saw how the horse beat its hoofs in the air, how it rose and ascended higher and higher, till it disappeared in the distance over the roofs of the houses. It was the devil who had turned himself into a horse to serve Faust.

The devil bore Faust through the air like a bird and fulfilled his every wish, no matter at what place or time.

After seven years the devil came into the house in the New Town not as a servant, but as a master. Now Faust belonged to him. He grasped him in his arms and flew out of the house with him through the ceiling. It is said that for a long time no one dared to tile over the burnt opening in the ceiling. And then, when one day they did tile it over, the next day the hole appeared again. It could not be closed.

Nor could the long line of Faust's wishes be closed.

After all those fulfilled wishes, the only wish that was left to Faust was to stay alive. Only that one single wish. The most important. And the one that could not be fulfilled.

The Student Who Made Magic

fter the devil had carried off Dr. Faust from the house in Charles' Square, that house remained empty. Nobody wanted to move into it, and as soon as it got dark people preferred not even to come near it...

The house was said to be haunted.

There was one student who was not afraid.

He had come to Prague from the country, he had no money to pay for a night's lodging. He thought he would stay in the deserted house - everyone was afraid of the house and he would be able to live there quietly.

He moved into the house. And he congratulated himself on having such a good idea. He lived there free and very comfortably too. The house was luxuriously furnished, everything remained as it had been in Dr. Faust's lifetime - beautiful furniture, a marble fireplace, a well-stocked library... In Faust's bedroom stood his canopied bed - unmade - just as the doctor had risen from it when the devil came for him. The student was not afraid, he was tired, so he lay down on the sorcerer's bed and slept and slept. How stupid people are, he said to himself, why are they afraid of this house? If the devil lived here, he would certainly not let me sleep so peacefully.

Next day he happily got up, got dressed...

Then he noticed that one of the slabs in the floor was sloping and he stamped it down. At that moment there was a great rumbling and the student stiffened in amazement. A stairway came down from the ceiling, and at the top of it was the entrance to a secret room. The stone slab had set an ingenious mechanism in motion... The student went up the stairway and found himself in a large room, full of vessels and retorts, all dusty and deserted since the moment when Dr. Faust had stopped working there. The student felt a breath of wind - he looked up and saw a hole in the ceiling. He understood. This was the very chamber from which, some years ago, the devil had carried off Faust's soul... There were books of magic lying all around. The student bent over their parchment, but he could not understand their mysterious records at all, so he ceased reading. He noticed a black stone bowl lying on the table and was delighted - in the bowl glittered a silver dollar, as if it had just been minted... The student did not think twice, he took the dollar and went out to eat in the town. It seemed to him that, from that moment, there was nothing to prevent his leading a contented life. There were plenty of things in the house that he would certainly be able to sell, so for some time there would be nothing for him to worry about, he could happily get on with his studies...

He lived in the house as if it had always belonged to him.

Every day he found a dollar in the black stone bowl, every day he took it. He never thought about who brought him that dollar in the empty house. Perhaps it was some good spirit. The student covered up the hole in the ceiling through which the devil had carried off Dr. Faust, so that chill should not penetrate the workroom, and did not worry about it any more. He was not hungry, he could buy himself lovely clothes or whatever he liked.

He even invited friends to the house.

He showed them all sorts of strange things that he had discovered in Faust's home. On the ground floor there was a mechanical drummer who started to drum as soon as anyone stepped on the paving stone beside him. In the overgrown garden, just by the entrance, there was a stone statue that squirted water when the student moved a lever in the wall and drenched anyone standing in front of it. On a great table made of green marble there sailed a little boat with oarsmen, as if the green table top were the surface of the sea...

His friends admired everything that the student showed them. But one thing he never told them: about the black bowl where every day a dollar glittered in the morning sun.

At first when he had found the dollar in the bowl he had told himself he would never be able to spend it.

But as he got used to his luxurious life, one dollar a day was too little for him. He decided to open the books that lay around in Faust's laboratory and would try and make magic, so that every day not one dollar would lie in the bowl, but several ducats.

He opened one of the books and began to call forth the devil.

When several days went by without the student's joining his friends in the tavern where he had so often drunk merrily with them, they decided to visit him.

They knocked on the gate, they tugged at the bellpull. They called the student.

The house was silent.

The friends walked round the house, climbed over the garden wall.

They entered the passage, the drummer drummed them a welcome, the notes of the drum echoed bleakly in the dusky passage.

They passed through the empty chambers to Faust's laboratory.

In that room everything was scattered about, as if a struggle had gone on there. Lying on the floor was a parchment book with the pages torn. Next to it an overturned candlestick with a black candle.

And everywhere the pungent smell of sulphur...

The friends felt a breath of wind on their cheeks - they looked up and saw a hole in the ceiling.

At that moment terror fell upon them, they rushed from the house.

They realised that their friend had called forth the evil spirit.

And he had flown off with him...

Again that gloomy house at the corner of the square lay empty for many years.

Stříbrná ryba u Myslíků.

The Fish

he legend of the silver fish has been told in Prague for centuries.

An ancient house used to stand at the corner of Myslíková and Spálená streets, and there lived a rich man of the name of Myslík.

After the Battle of the White Mountain this man with his whole family had to escape from Bohemia - and how many families left their native Bohemia even in later centuries...

Before he left Prague he piled into a heap all the silver he had in the house.

Then he melted it down and poured all the silver into a huge earthenware mould in the form of a fish, a mould they had used in the kitchen.

Into this mould he poured the silver from jewels, from cutlery, candlesticks and from richly ornamented goblets - from everything he had to leave, that he could not carry with him as he fled.

Then he walled up the big silver fish.

For generations it rested in the wall of his house.

The house became old and dilapidated and the city councillors ordered the new owner to pull down the house, as it was a danger to passers-by, and to build a new one in its place.

But how was he to do that , when he had no money?

He had nothing, just the old ruined house...

He was completely at a loss...

Where was he to find the money for a new house?

But he began to demolish the house.

And then the bricklayers discovered the great silver fish walled up in the old wall.

The house-owner was no longer worried as to how to build his new house.

He sold the fish and for what he got for it he had a big new house built on the site of that of the unhappy Mr. Myslík.

So the silver fish floated through centuries and in the end helped someone who needed it.

And the silver fish is still floating in a legend that gives hope: fate knows how to help anyone it wants to, and always just at the right moment.

The ill luck of one becomes the good luck of another.

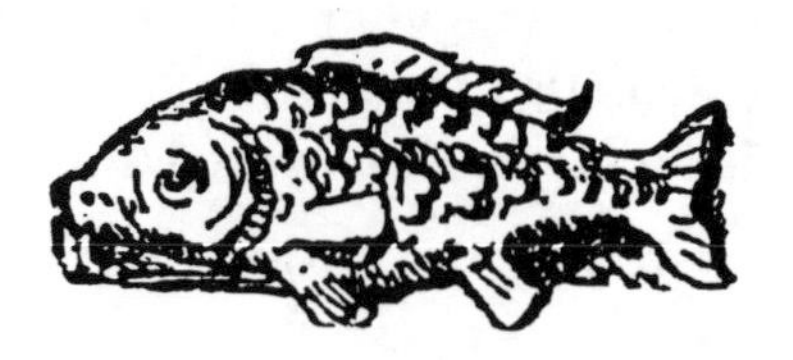

Cert co
kuchař
w
klášteře
Emauském
1905.

The Devil a Cook

When Charles IV., King of Bohemia and Roman Emperor, built the New Town he founded a monastery there in which the services were held in the ancient manner, in the Slav language...

At that time there were many merchants from the Slav countries in Bohemia, many strangers lived here and the king remembered them, knowing they were used to religious services in their own tongue. They did not understand Latin, as was used for services in Prague.

As the church was consecrated on Easter Monday, when the gospel is read during mass about Jesus appearing in Emmaus, not only the church but the monastery too was given the name Emmaus.

As it was said that particularly godly monks lived in this monastery, the devil decided that he would set out to lure them to an evil life.

One day the queue in front of the monastery was joined by a new cook - the monks did not know it was the devil who had taken on human form... And so they let him look after the kitchen for them.

Perhaps nowhere in Prague did people eat so well as in the Emmaus monastery in those days. Such delicious smells were wafted from the monastery kitchen, as if the cook there was not preparing meals for monks, but delicacies for the royal table.

The monks, who grew used to this splendid food, grew lazy and fat, they didn't want to get up to worship and to live as monks should. The cook had not even expected that he would achieve what he longed for so speedily through his art.

But it came about that one night the Abbot was walking past the kitchen where the devil cooked. That night the devil had a guest, another devil, who had come up from hell to see how the plot was working. Just as the Abbot passed the kitchen door the devilish cook was relating his successes to his friend. Frightful laughter burst out of the kitchen and reached the Abbot's ears. The Abbot heard everything and was horrified.

Next day he waited for the cook.

"Depart from our monastery, unclean spirit!" he shouted at him, raising a cross as a weapon.

At that moment there was a gush of flame, the devil turned into a fiery cock, jumped on the sill of the open window, flapped his wings - and flew away.

Nothing any longer prevented the monks from again devoting themselves to their austere lives...

And the Emmaus monastery won back its reputation as a famous place and the home of godly monks.

The Church called Na Karlově

or centuries a legend has been handed down about the church that Charles IV. built on the edge of the New Town and which is called after him "Karlov" - Charles's.

At the time when the building of this church was only being considered a young builder lived in Prague who wanted to marry the New Town Mayor's daughter. But the mayor would not give his consent until his future son-in-law grew rich. So when the young man heard that it had not yet been decided who should build Charles's church he started drawing plans. Then he set out with them to see the emperor, who liked the plans and chose the young builder to direct the building of the new church - and he got down to work immediately. He knew he would not easily find again such an opportunity to win fame and money - and the girl he loved.

He had designed for the church an arch so daring that no one in Prague had ever seen its like. And people prophesied that the church must collapse.

Especially those builders whom the emperor had refused, swore it was impossible for the church not to collapse.

The emperor summoned the young builder to court.

"I believe in you. I am sure the builders who slander your work are wrong - but see that you do not disappoint me."

The young builder began to doubt himself - perhaps it was impossible for such a splendid arch to endure.

And then he was visited by the devil. He promised that the building would succeed, that the builder would achieve his every desire - if only he would sign over his soul to him. He handed the builder a parchment. The builder did not even glance to see what was written there. At that moment he would have sacrificed everything for success. The devil took up a pair of compasses and pricked the builder's left hand, a few drops of blood spurted out. He dipped a raven's quill into this blood and gave it to the builder. He signed without hesitation. The devil disappeared. The builder did not know if it was a dream or if he had really signed over his soul to hell.

He set to work enthusiastically and soon the whole magnificent work was completed.

But the brick-layers were terribly afraid for the unusual building - they refused to pull down the scaffolding that supported the arch. They believed that when they dismantled the scaffolding under the arch, the church would come crashing down on them. Then, as the builder could not persuade the brick-layers, it occurred to him that he could burn the scaffolding - then it would fall down by itself.

The scaffolding blazed up and the arch of the church became a vault of fire.

The young builder gazed at the conflagration and it was as if he were gazing into the gorge of hell.

The scaffolding burnt through and fell to the ground, the flames leapt up and the clatter of the burning beams drowned the voice of the terrified people.

The builder took fright. Hell has surely deceived me, he thought, and he ran from the church to the river Vltava, hurled himself into its waves and drowned.

Meanwhile the scaffolding had all fallen and was smouldering on the ground.

The magnificent arch of Charles's church rose boldly to the blue sky...

The emperor himself came to look at the Karlov church and was amazed at it beauty.

He commanded that the young builder should be brought to him as he wished to decorate him.

Only the next day Prague fishermen found the body of the drowned builder who had not believed in his work.

His work has endured for centuries and is enchanting still...

The Treasure of Poříčí

Once a rich man lived in Na Poříčí who loved nothing but his money. When he died his relations all gathered and dreamt of the immense wealth they would find. But the treasures they hoped to inherit had disappeared...

For a long time they searched all the places where they thought he might have hidden his treasure, but they found nothing...

They buried the miser.

Some time afterwards the Poříče sexton noticed that at midnight a glimmering little light hovered over the graveyard.

He investigated which grave the little light came from - and found it was the miser's grave.

He went to find his son, the gravedigger, and showed him the light.

The gravedigger would at once have taken a spade and started digging in the miser's grave, but the sexton stopped him.

"As soon as you start digging the treasure - if its there - would fall into the earth, and you would never dig it up. There is just one chance of our getting hold of that treasure. We must get a big rosary and lie in wait with it at midnight by that glimmering grave... It is said that you must throw the rosary onto the grave so that the little flame is caught in the middle of the rosary. Only then can the treasure be dug up at that place."

And so at midnight that is what they did.

As soon as the rosary was tossed over the flame, the flame stiffened and didn'n move any more.

They dug for a while and when they found the coffin they opened it.

1902

Beneath the dead man the coffin was filled with jewels and coins. The rich man had not wanted to part with his possessions even after death, and he thought he would succeed in taking them with him to the grave.

The sexton and the gravedigger did not keep the treasure for themselves, but gave it away to the poor, and so the miser's money did much good.

The Spring of St. Wenceslas

Not far from the Church of St. Wenceslas in Resslová Street there used to be an ancient well. People came from far and wide to this well, and they believed that its water would give them health.

It is told that at the time when the extensive territory of present-day Prague was covered by deep forest, Prince Wenceslas, who was declared a saint after his death, one day went out hunting. He rode through the place where later Charles IV. founded the New Town. Where today we hear the noise of cars and the clatter of trams, the fanfares of hunting horns resounded...

Prince Wenceslas is said to have liked particularly riding on this bank of the river Vltava, opposite Prague Castle.

One day the hounds announced that they had tracked down their prey, the prince heard their barking and went to meet them. A stag leapt out of the bushes and ran with all its might away from the following pack.

The prince rode after the stag, the stag stumbled.

As his hoof glanced off a root, he fell to the ground. But at once he jumped up and ran on. The prince noticed that the stag had rolled a stone away from the ground, and beneath it a spring appeared.

The prince told his company to let the stag escape.

He bent over the spring and ordered that a well should be dug where the spring bubbled up. The water that Prince Wenceslas had captured instead of the stag had a delicious taste, was crystal clear and curative.

Thus the prince gave its life to the stag and the well to many people.

PRAMEN SV: VÁCLAVA.
Aleš

The Builder of the Charles Bridge

It is said that when King Wenceslas IV. had St. John of Nepomuk thrown from the Charles Bridge an arch of the bridge at that place also fell that night.

And no one was able to mend the bridge. They tried many times, but as soon as they had walled up the bridge, again for a moment - it crashed down again. Then came a builder who said he could easily fix it. He came from abroad, where he had gained experience, and he had no doubt that he could build the arch. He kept watch overnight to make sure the bridge did not fall - but as he was standing by the Bridge Tower he heard a rumbling - even he had not been able to build an arch at that place.

He stood desolately on the bridge and stared into the darkness.

An then some one spoke to him.

The devil.

"I am the only one who can help you, builder."

"Do you want my soul?" asked the frightened builder, he knew that the devil took human souls for his aid.

"Not at all," said the devil. "It will be enough for me to have the one who first walks over the vault of the arch you build!"

The builder thought for a moment, then he smiled and nodded, he could easily agree to that.

He decided that as soon as the bridge was built he would let a cock run across it - then the devil could take that to hell.

Really the stonemasons' work went so well, as if hell were helping them.

The builder had both bridge towers guarded, so that no one could cross the bridge.

But the devil took on the likeness of a stonemason and ran to the builder's wife. He told her she should run to the Charles Bridge to help her husband, who had been injured in an accident.

The wife ran through the bridge gateway and hastened to her husband. The people who were guarding the bridge knew her and let her through.

When she found that nothing had happened to her husband she was overjoyed.

But her husband was struck dumb.

He understood.

In the grip of horror he went to the celebration of the reopening of the bridge and kept waiting to see what would happen.

When he came home after the ceremony he found a still-born child, who had been born just at the time when the bridge was opened - and his wife, who was dying...

And above his head the builder heard the rustle of the devil's wings.

The Haughty·Lady

Once there was a tradeswoman in Prague who sold poultry, buying the birds from country women who brought them to Prague.

It happened that a woman from Jílové came and offered her some hens. The tradeswoman bought them and, as she wanted to have a hen for lunch herself that day, she killed one of those she had just bought. But when she came to prepare it for cooking she was astonished. She found gold in the hen's stomach. Then she found grains of gold in the stomachs of the other hens from Jílové. She had heard tell that gold used to be obtained from the ground in Jílové, and she presumed that the hens brought her little nuggets and grains of gold in their stomachs from the old sites where it had been found. She agreed with the woman from Jílové that she would not sell her hens and chickens to anybody else - only to her - and she gaily got richer.

She bought a big house, she built little shops in Prague for tradesmen and craftsmen - she built a famous place where people sold things in Prague for centuries and which was given the name Kotce, meaning Huts. She bought a whole estate and a mansion.

She drove about in a splendid coach and she had no sympathy for poor people...

One day she was taking a walk across the Charles Bridge and sitting in the middle of the bridge she saw a beggar.

He begged her for alms - but she turned her eyes away.

The beggar said to her: "May you, my lady, never have to beg one day as I have to."

The lady turned haughtily to the beggar. She drew off her glove, took a precious ring from her finger and threw it into the river Vltava. She laughed and looked triumphantly at the beggar.

"As I shall never see this ring again, so your words that I might beg will never come true!"

Next day the lady was giving a banquet at her house. And then she was called to the kitchen - the servants said something unheard-of had happened. She hurried to the kitchen, where the cook was bending over a large pike. When he saw the lady he handed her a golden ring that he had found in the fish...

"My lady, you are lucky in everything. Even fish bring you treasures."

The haughty lady turned pale.

It was the ring she had thrown into the Vltava the previous day.

"What awaits me now?" she thought, "certainly nothing good..."

And indeed, from that moment one catastrophe overtook her after another. She received news that her mansion had burnt down. Thieves visited her house and took all they could carry. A tradesman she got in touch with cheated her.

She fell ill, and when she could no longer look after her affairs her trade fell off...

Could the beggar on the bridge that day have been right? she asked herself...

She had to sell all the things that surrounded her, one after another, and at every sale she remembered the beggar.

How glad she would have been now to fill his hat full of ducats. If only she could take her words back...

The last thing that remained to her was the ring. The one that had come back to her in the pike's stomach.

But she had to part even with that ring that she had thrown over the side of the bridge.

This time she did not part with it haughtily - she sold it sadly to a goldsmith, who had no idea what memories were linked with that ring.

Nothing was left to her.

She walked through Prague, where for so many years she had driven in a carriage, and wondered what she should do now.

Again she remembered that old man on the bridge...

She went to have a look at him.

But the place where he had sat was empty.

The lady hesitated.

Then she sat down in the place where that old man had sat.

She looked round timidly. And held out a pleading hand.

People passed by and no one gave her even the smallest coin.

But then one man...

He bent and placed a coin in those fingers that had been adorned with so many precious rings.

Today you can still find in Prague the little street called The Huts (V Kotcích). For generations tradesmen have had their goods spread out on one open counter next to another. And maybe they have no idea that they are following in the footsteps of those who sold their goods there centuries ago.

About Master Hanuš

Since distant times there has been a beautiful horologe on the Town Hall of the Old Town, a clock that people came from far to see, both Czechs and foreigners visiting Prague.

But towards the end of the fifteenth century Master Hanuš lived in Prague, a famous clock-maker, who added three new parts to the old clock, thus making a horologe or astronomical clock unparallelled in the whole of Europe.

Today people can still admire this splendid clock, a memorial to the most famous of Czech clock-makers. On it they can tell the daytime and the night-time hours, both according to solar or to stellar time. The clock shows the days and the months, it shows the rising and the setting of the sun and the moon, the waxing and waning of the moon, the position of the earth towards the sun and the moon. The spectator may see on the horologe the course of the planets and the signs of the zodiac. There is a calendar too, that shows the date of every day... Two windows over the clockface open every hour, behind them pass the figures of Jesus and the twelve apostles, looking down upon the square. As soon as this procession has gone a cock crows, a little statue in another window. It flaps its wings. There are other figures too on this famous astronomical clock. - There is the skeleton of Death, who turns over an hourglass, opens gaping jaws, nods his head and rings a bell, to draw the spectator's attention to the end of their lives. Next to Death stands the figure of a Turk - he shakes his head to show Death that he does not wish to leave the world yet. There is the figure of a miser on the clock too. He rattles a moneybag, as a sign of the vanity of amassing a fortune. The figure of a profligate gazes into a mirror. Generation after generation comes to the Old Town clock...

It is told how once there used to be a prison in the Old Town and a prisoner who had lost hope that his dispute would end well looked from his prison window - at the figure of the skeleton.

And he saw how a sparrow flew into the skeleton's open mouth and nestled down there.

But then Death snapped its jaws and the sparrow was imprisoned between its gums.

The prisoner took this to be an evil omen.

He would remain imprisoned for ever.

Or would he even be beheaded?

Death had shown him clearly what fate awaited him - it had caught him firmly, like the sparrow, in its mouth.

The prisoner fell prey to hopelessness and gazed dismally at the sparrow, flailing wildly, clenched fast in the bony jaws of death...

I too am imprisoned, just as he is...

But the next hour, when the mechanism of the clock started to move again, the jaws opened and the sparrow flew out of the mouth of death. This again the prisoner saw as a good omen: and he was not wrong - his dispute ended well and he was able to leave the Old Town prison, to go out as a free man...

It is told how the aldermen of the Old Town feared that Master Hanuš might betray the secret of the best clock in the world. They were not sure whether someone would not bribe him, and the great clock-maker would not construct a similar astronomical clock in some other city, and Prague would thus lose its unique wonder...

So they blinded the master clock-maker.

Master Hanuš learnt who had done this, and decided that he would have his revenge on the aldermen.

He wished to visit his horologe once more - once more to hear the clatter of its wheels, to touch the amazing mechanism...

Whom have I harmed?

Why have they so harmed me?

He went into the horologe with his helper, he listened to the regular ticking of his work… he took his leave of it.

He put his hand into the horologe

He grasped one of the levers and moved it.

Then the helper bent over his master, but he did not hear his breath, at the moment when he had destroyed his machine, his heart broke.

Master Hanuš had stopped the mechanism at the moment when it was in motion, when the figure of Death tolled its bell.

At that sign the horologe stopped.

No one knew then how to set the clock going again, and it took a long time before another clock-maker could mend it.

So anyway the aldermen lost their horologe for a long, long time.

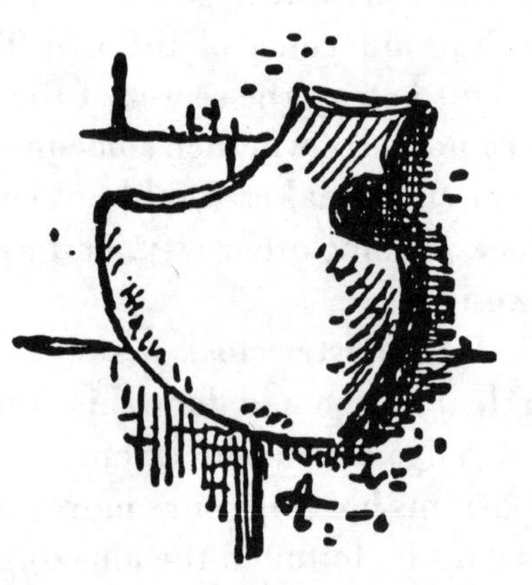

Zuzana

he Czech lords were dissatisfied with King Wenceslas IV., who surrounded himself with his favourites and listened to their advice. So they lay in wait for him along the way where he rode with his courtiers, and took him prisoner. Legend says they held him captive in the Town Hall of the Old Town.

Weeks passed and the king did not want to give in and retreat from his method of government, and the Czech lords did not want to retreat either.

The hot breath of summer descended on Prague, it was retained between the walls of the houses and the sky did not cease to glow.

Then the king said to his guards:

"Go to your commanders and tell them: Your king desires to bathe, give him the possibility to visit the baths."

The guards delivered the king's message and those who had the king in their power decided that they should allow him a bath. And it was laid down that the king should go to the nearest baths, those by the Stone Bridge, that he should go in simple clothing, and that he should be escorted on the way by four guards, who would not allow him to deflect from the shortest path.

The king went to the baths with his guards, he bathed, but the warm water did not refresh him much. So he asked if he could go out from the baths onto a wooden landing-stage to breathe the evening air. The guards agreed, the landing-state led nowhere and the king had no clothes, just a piece of linen, with which he had dried himself and had wound round his body.

The king stepped out of the baths onto the landing-state and allowed himself to be greeted by the evening breeze that was hurrying across the river. He looked up from the landing-stage to the darkening heavens, with long rays of sun, and to the royal castle, from which he had been expelled for weeks, and his gaze returned to the river. The birds circled freely over it in the setting sun, and in the freedom of their wings the king read his own yearning for freedom. He looked around him, whether he could not somewhere see a way to freedom for himself.

At that moment there came out of the baths a young woman who helped there.

"Listen," the king addressed her, "don t you know some way out of here? If you quickly help me to get to the other bank, I will reward you as only a king can. But hurry, hurry, before those men come out of the baths to take me away again."

The woman knew who it was standing before her, and understood. She pointed in silence to the end of the landing-stage. And she climbed down over the beams beneath the stage to where a boat was tied up. The king followed her. They got in quietly, the woman pulled at the oars and the boat shot out with the current of the river towards the other bank. In spirit the king wondered at the sturdy oarswoman, but he said nothing aloud. He was watching the wooden landing-state, that was receding into the distance. The guards were still at leisure in the baths.

They landed on the other bank and hastily set out across the meadows to Chuchle. They hid behind thickets, but before long they were hidden by darkness.

"Tell me, what is your name?" the king asked the young woman.

"They call me Zuzana," she replied.

"The stars that are coming out above us are my witness," said the king, "that I shall never forget the service you have done me."

As night fell they arrived in Chuchle and Zuzana roused up the ferryman. The ferryman hesitated and looked suspiciously at the king's strange apparel. But the silver that Zuzana pressed into his hand awoke a different, grateful surprise. He hurried willingly to his ferry and took the king and Zuzana across the river. The shore on which they landed meant ransom for the king. Here in the forest stood his New Castle, with a garrison faithful to the king.

The king knew his forest well, as he loved hunting there. He chose the shortest path and even in the middle of the night reached the castle moat with his companion. The drawbridge was drawn up and they had to shout to call the guard and convince him that the man standing across the moat, barefoot and barely clothed, was the Bohemian king. They let down the bridge and the burgrave himself came out with men-at-arms, who lit the darkness with torches for him. He recognised that the man was indeed the king.

Joyfully he led his master into the palace. He had a sumptuous supper prepared for the king and his companion and suitable garments. The king appeared at the royal table in a splendid robe. For Zuzana too a noblewoman's dress was found. There they sat, opposite one another in the banqueting-hall, the rescued man with his rescuer, they laughed and recalled their escape like the best of friends. After a ceremonial toast the king ordered the burgrave to bring a pouch with a hundred ducats. He handed the pouch with the ducats to Zuzana:

"Take this," he said, "it is my return for what you paid for me at the ferry."

And it is said that King Wenceslas IV. took over the government again, and did not forget Zuzana. He had new baths built by the bridge in place of the old ones, and gave them to her in gratitude for saving him, and in addition he dedicated to her an annual income of twenty heaps of groshes. Zuzana's deed brought good to other bath attendants too. The king remembered them in a decree that promoted them to the same standard as other crafts.

The Three Golden Roses

The Little Square, which one reaches in a few moments' walk from the Old Town horologe, is linked with a strange story.

Legend tells that on the site of the house where Rott's ironmongery now is, there once lived three beautiful sisters. These sisters where too much aware of their beauty and they refused one suitor after another. They were very rich girls, but their riches did not bring them calm and content. They quarrelled amongst themselves from morning to evening...

Beauty is too often linked with pride.

The people of Prague used to say that these three proud sisters would grow old quarrelling and would die spinsters, despite their wealth and beauty.

But then a foreigner rang the bell of their house.

A beautiful exotic prince.

He declared that he had fallen in love with the oldest of the three sisters and he did everything to win her love.

It didn't give him much trouble, the eldest sister was glad that she overshadowed her younger sisters, and so she was pleased to believe that the foreigner's love for her was sincere - and that she would live abroad with him in luxury. She understood from the foreigner's splendid clothes and from what he told her that his property was far greater than hers.

She went away with him to his unknown country.

After a time the bell rang again at the house of the two sisters who had remained at home. Again it was a foreigner who rang. He proclaimed that he was an Englishman and that he had fallen in love with the middle sister. He could not live without her - and if she could learn to love him, he offered her a happy life in plenty abroad.

The middle sister did not hesitate for long, ever since the oldest one had married she had envied her.

Now she would be able to equal her... and maybe her bridegroom was even richer.

Before long the people of Prague looked on as she drove away from her house with the foreigner.

The third sister remained in the house. The youngest.

She walked about the empty house and remembered her two sisters with hatred. After all, they were not nearly so pretty as I am, and they were older - she said to herself - how unjust it is that such rich foreigners fell in love just with them, and I have to stay here in this old house all alone...

She looked in the mirror and was afraid of old age.

Then one day the bell of that house tinkled again...

She looked out of the window and her heart leapt up - again a foreigner stood before the door and again he was magnificently clothed.

Perhaps he has come for me...

She longed for it to be true, she longed to have the same good luck as her sisters.

And it seemed she was not wrong...

The foreigner who entered the house and spoke of having fallen in love with her, was a cavalier at first sight.

What a pity, the youngest sister said to herself, that my sisters are not here, they would certainly both of them envy me this rich bridegroom.

He told her that he came from the land of France, that he was a nobleman and his possessions were immense.

The youngest sister fell in love with him straight away.

I shall no longer have to live in this empty house and get cross when I think what good luck my sisters had and how I was left all alone.

Should she go away with him?

She did not hesitate.

Again the people of Prague saw a gorgeous coach, piled with luggage, drive away from the Little Square, again they saw a smiling girlish face at its window.

The house in the Little Square was silent for a long time.

And people remembered the beautiful sisters, many remembered them with yearning, many a young man's heart was sick for their beauty.

It happened that after some time news came to Prague of the fate of the three sisters...

And it was terrible news.

Nothing else was talked of in Prague for a long time...

It was not three bridegrooms who had taken away the three beauties - all of them had one single bridegroom. A man who knew very well how to disguise himself and could change his voice, had decided to appropriate the great property of all three sisters.

Three times had he entered their house and three times had he led one of them away.

They had been too dazed with the longing to outshine the other sisters and did not notice the seducer's insidiousness.

The end of those three sisters was a sad one.

The swindler had robbed them of their dream and of their fortune. He deserted them in poverty and before long, one after another, they died in distant lands.

What remained of them?

A story.

And the name of the house At the Sign of Three Golden Roses, the name of the house they lived in and that people gave it in memory of those three unhappy girls.

Rotlev

he Carolinum, the building that now belongs to Charles University, was not always university property. This splendid house has an interesting history...

Once there lived in Prague a burgher named Rotlev - a rich burgher. He owned several Prague houses, gardens and vineyards. But he wanted to be richer still, so he obtained mining rights. He started prospecting for gold near Jílové. The miners he hired searched diligently for the precious metal. In all the galleries opened up by others gold came to the surface, but just the gallery that Rotlev opened up was bare of gold-bearing ore... The miners' wages gradually swallowed up Rotlev's fortune and the profit from work in the mine was tiny: even if a vein of gold did appear it was so poor that it soon gave out.

Rotlev sold house after house, vineyard after vineyard.

Rotlev's wife tried to persuade him, warning him that he was burying the family prosperity in the Jilové mine.

But Rotlev would not listen to her.

He refused to see that beggary was staring him in the face, but clung to the belief that in the end he would be rich.

He hadn't even enough to pay the miner's wages. He promised he would pay them, but could not just now...

An old servant came to Rotlev on horseback from Jílové and told him the miners had stopped work, they wanted to go and complain of him to the Prague aldermen.

But he also told Rotlev about his dream. He had been visited by a sprite, who pointed out one certain place in the gallery. When the old servant woke up he had wanted to tell the miners to dig at that place - but they had already stopped work. So he had ridden to see Rotlev, to tell him of his dream.

What could the sprite have wanted to tell him when he pointed to the rockface?

It was quite clear to Rotlev: The sprite had pointed to where he could find gold.

And the Prague burgher had no one who would lend him the money to dig... So Rotlev took his wife's wedding veil, a veil threaded with gold threads and adorned with pearls. The last valuable object he had at home and that his wife did not wish to sell.

He borrowed against this wedding veil and set off with the money for Jílové. He paid the miners and begged them to be sure and come to work next day.

But he could not wait till morning.

He went into the gallery in the dark and tried to continue work at the place the sprite had pointed out.

The work did not go well, it seemed the dream had lied...

Rotlev sat sadly in the light of a tallow pit lamp. And as he sat there he noticed a mouse trying to drag off a bit of tallow prepared for lighting.

Rotlev was seized by long suppressed rage.

Even that mouse wants to steal from me, he thought.

He grabbed a miners' sledge and threw it at the mouse.

He didn't hit it, the sledge broke off a bit of stone from the gallery.

And Rotlev saw in the light of the pit lamp that something started to glimmer at that place...

He held the lamp up to the glimmer - and was filled with fear that he would wake up and find it was all a dream: in the flickering light he saw a vein of gold.

From that moment Rotlev's fate changed.

Again he became one of Prague's rich men. The first thing he did when money began to pour in from his rich gold mine, was to reclaim his wife's wedding veil or mantilla, as it was called. Rotlev gave the name Mantilla to the mine in which he had again found fortune, in memory of a stroke of luck and of his own persistence.

Then he rebuilt his Old Town house, which was one of the most beautiful in the city.

In the reign of King Wenceslas IV. a university college moved into this house... and since that day it has been part of Charles University.

The Prague Red Indians

he house At the Sign of The Three Wild Men in Provaznická Street in the Old Town owes its strange name to the first visit of Red Indians in Bohemia.

And the first Red Indians in Bohemia were CZECH RED INDIANS.

An English speculator came to Prague with a remarkable attraction, from which he hoped for much. He came with Red Indians. At that time everything connected with America sounded incredible in Bohemia - the New World was as exotic for the people of old Prague as sci-fi stories have become for those of modern Prague. Almost as if the Red Indians had not come to Bohemia from America, but from the most distant planet...

The hall of one of the old Prague houses was sold out at every performance, and the Englishman happily reckoned the profit that his Prague tour was bringing in.

An old farmer came into the hall where the Red Indians were performing. He came from Vodňany in south Bohemia. He wanted to see all he could in Prague, and could well imagine how they would listen in astonishment at home when he told them he had seen real Red Indians in the capital of the kingdom...

He sat down in the hall and looked at the Red Indians. They were leaping about the stage, dressed in skins and feathers, they were terrifyingly painted with coloured clay, like Red Indians on the warpath. They danced wild Red Indian dances and sang Red Indian songs. The Prague people were especially amazed that the American Indians ate raw meat on the stage... They really were proper wild men...

Then the old farmer from south Bohemia shouted:

"Honzík!" (Something like Jackie.)

A
1903.

One of the Red Indians looked round startled.

And the old man called the other Indians by name too.

He knew them all, even though he had never been in America - and he began to explain to the surprised audience that he knew all three of them well - they were from the Liběјice court, but they had been thrown out because they stole, and the thieves had become tramps.

What could the English speculator do?

Hastily end the performance and run away with the Prague Indians as quickly as he could.

The disgrace of it was talked about all over Prague.

And lots of people thought about whom they had admired... thinking things over is very useful...

All that has remained of the whole story is the legend and the name.

At the Sign of the Three Wild Men, that is what the old house has been called ever since. And that name has remained.

The Prisoner in the Little Quarter

t is told that when St. Wenceslas was murdered in Stará Boleslav they brought his body to Prague Castle.

When the cart with the saint's body reached the Little Quarter Square it stopped, and whatever the driver did the cart would not move.

Many people gathered around the cart, they helped and gave advice, but not one of them managed to get the cart moving again. The white oxen that were harnessed exerted all their strength when the whip cracked over them, but the cart stood as if turned into a stone in the ground. They harnessed several more pairs of oxen, but however many they added, still the cart did not stir from its place. Then a priest passed by the cart, thought a moment and gave the carter some good advice.

"When Prince Wenceslas was alive, he could not tolerate anyone's suffering injustice, and I am sure he does not want to tolerate it even after death. You notice that the cart stopped in front of the Little Quarter prison. There must be someone in that prison who is innocent."

They judged it would be best to bring all the prisoners out of the prison and investigate whether there was not one among them who really had been unjustly condemned.

At that time there were only three prisoners in the Little Quarter prison.

When they took them out they led them in front of the cart on which the dead saint lay.

A clangour was heard.

The chains had fallen from the hands and the feet of one of the prisoners.

And at that moment the white oxen pulled and the cart with the saint's body moved forward...

1903

They at once examined why the prisoner whose chains had miraculously fallen from his hands and feet had been imprisoned. And they found that indeed he had been wrongfully accused.

The other two prisoners were astounded at this miracle and wanted immediately to take the christian faith.

So even after his death St. Wenceslas brought souls to God. The chains that had fallen from the hands and feet of the innocent prisoner, and two bits of wood from the cart, were long honoured and Emperor Charles IV. had them laid in the Karlštejn chapel of St. Catherine.

The Hunger Wall

here have been times in Bohemia when the land was flowing with gold and awoke the envy of other nations, times when it seemed that prosperity would never fade, but then too there have been times when war or a bad harvest afflicted the Bohemian kingdom so bitterly that its people had not even the money for bread...

Once during the reign of Emperor Charles IV. lean years came upon the land, food was immensely expensive. Those were days when people did not steal for greed, they stole bread - so that they should not die.

The prisons were full of the desperate poor...

And the king of Bohemia asked his courtiers:

"Do you think it is better to die of hunger or to steal bread?"

The courtiers thought it over.

"We think it is bad to steal, but it is better than dying of hunger."

The emperor replied: "In my kingdom people will neither have to steal nor go hungry."

And he thought how he could help his nation. Once when he was coming out of church, a great crowd of Czech people gathered. They begged the king for work - as they had no way to earn bread for their families.

And the king promised that he would see to it.

He initiated the building of an enormous wall that was to protect the city, a wall that started at the royal castle and went across the hill slopes to the Vltava. A wall that was to protect Prague for future generations.

Even today you can see the remains of this famous wall on Petřín Hill.

For two years, as long as the poverty lasted, Charles IV. had this wall built, but none of those who built it received pay: only food, clothes, boots.

The wall was called the Hunger Wall.

The top of the wall did not end in a straight line but, as was the medieval custom, in an indented or toothed one. And it was said in Bohemia that these "teeth" were there for eternal memory. They were a reminder of how Charles IV. took care that his poor people's teeth should have something to bite into.

The sovereign used to come to Petřín to see the builders and observe the building growing - to see how his people lived, whom he called his family.

There have been few sovereigns in Bohemia for whom their nation, the Czechs, was their family.

That was how the wise Charles IV. turned the poverty of his subjects into a great memorial that adorned the city and helped to defend it from its enemies for many a long year.

The Ball

nce upon a time famous balls were held in the Lichtenštejn Palace. Every woman in Prague had heard of them, and there were many who would have given anything just to be able to dance at those balls.

The daughter of the greatest of the Little Quarter millers was one who longed very much to be able to dance at the ball, and one day, as she was brushing her hair in front of the mirror, she said aloud that she would even give her soul to the devil if only she could get to that famous ball.

Ever since childhood she had seen magnificent coaches driving to the palace, had seen lords and ladies descending from them, had heard music from the gleaming windows of the palace.

The world she imagined existed in the palace had enchanted her for years, and indeed it seemed to her like paradise.

Soon after she had expressed her wish in front of the mirror, a liveried servant came to the mill and brought her an invitation to the ball.

Her father was a rich man, but all the same it was all she could do to get as much money out of him as she wanted for a resplendent dress - for she had determined to be queen of the ball. At last her parents decided that they could spend the money on the dress - what if their daughter won a bridegroom at the famous ball... The dress she had made was delicious, she stood for a long time in front of the mirror and turned to look at herself from all sides - no princess can be as beautiful as I am, she thought to herself.

The only thing that worried her was what jewels she should wear. The ones she had seemed to her too poor for such a famous ball, and she knew that her father, having protested at paying for the dress, would not buy her any new jewels.

Then, when she was getting quite desperate about it, the servant who had brought her the invitation came to the mill again. This time he brought a casket, with which he said his master had sent him to the miller's daughter. Who his master was he didn't say. But he asked her to sign a receipt that she had really received the casket.

She signed, without even looking to see what it was she was signing.

When the servant had gone, she hastily opened the casket - a brilliant glitter flashed from it: in the casket lay the most magnificent necklace she had ever seen. The diamonds in it shone like little suns.

Some nobleman must have fallen in love with me, thought the miller's daughter.

When she came to the palace that evening, she saw the blaze of the windows from afar, and she was happier than she had ever been in her life.

None of the women who were dancing in the hall had such a splendid dress as she had, none had such a splendid necklace.

She entered the dance hall, the band started playing a minuet.

And standing in front of her was a dancing partner, he bowed - and they started to dance. He must be the one who sent me the necklace, and surely he is in love with me. She gazed at him enchanted. Perhaps he is a Spanish nobleman, there are so many of them in Prague now... She half closed her eyes and the hall dissolved into a single golden blur.

During the dance her partner was stubbornly silent.

He's probably shy, she thought.

After the dance her partner drew a slip of paper from his pocket and handed it to her. Perhaps he doesn't know our language, it crossed her mind, and she bent coquettishly over the note. Surely there would be some passionate confession of love written there. But what she saw was her own signature -

and when she read what was written over it, she screamed. It was the receipt she had signed when she had received the necklace for the ball from the servant. Her signature had not confirmed that she had taken a necklace from the servant, she read in terror what it was she had signed... that she would give her soul to the devil. She looked up in fear and met the eyes of the dancer standing beside her -he smiled triumphantly...

She screamed.

And at that moment her heart stopped in horror.

The guests gathered round her, looking amazed at the dead girl in the most magnificent dress, as she lay on the floor and her face was distorted with immense fear.

The dancer who had whirled with her in the minuet was not there... he had disappeared.

Her mother, the miller's wife, pushed her way through the crowd standing round the body and bent over her daughter... When she saw that she was dead, she fainted. The coach that had brought them to the brightly lit palace now took them back into darkness.

Ever since that night the ghost of the unhappy girl has appeared in the Lichtenštejn Palace, she walks through the halls she dreamed of when she was alive... How often just the fulfilment of a dream may send a soul to hell.

The King and the Stars

ing Wenceslas was seized by confusion and doubt and anxiety about his future. Legend relates that at such black moments he had his court astrologer summoned.

"You know how to read the stars," said the king, "read what is written about me there. And give me a report, whether good or bad."

The astrologer asked for time, and the whole night he observed the sky and calculated and turned the pages of thick volumes. In the morning he came before the king.

"I have but one single piece of news for you, my king," he said. "It is written in the stars that you will die before the spire of St. Vitus."

"Tell me," shouted the king, "who is scheming against me, shall I die by the sword?"

"There is nothing about that in the stars," replied the astrologer.

"Or perhaps," the king wondered, "the spire is to fall upon me?"

But the astrologer could not answer that either.

"Ye gods," the petulant king grew angry, "what dumb stars did you choose for your prophesy?"

From that moment Wenceslas IV. became captive to the thought of his own end, he was his own captive. And no friend could enter into that captivity, and no boat could carry him to a shore where safety and calm should await him. He gave wide berth to the spire of the church that was in building, but the thought of the spire he could not avoid.

He summoned the astrologer again.

"I shall leave Prague Castle," he told him, "but before I go I shall issue an order that the spire is to be demolished. What do you say to that? If the spire disappears, I cannot die before it.

And I shall not return until it is razed to the ground."

"There is nothing about that in the stars," replied the astrologer.

"Those stars of yours," the king laughed and waved a hand. He was in a good mood again, pleased with his idea.

That same day he left for his New Castle, almost as care-free as when he used to go there.

But in the old, well-known places of the New Castle he tried in vain to recall all the happy moments he had spent there. In the meantime at Prague Castle the workmen obeyed the king's order. They started to demolish the spire, but they were in no hurry. They carried out disbelievingly what they had been charged to do - not able to understand that they should destroy the work that had grown under their hands.

A horseman put an end to their uncertainty and to the destruction of the spire. He galloped helter-skelter to the New Castle on the last day but one of the month of July, at the hour when shadows begin to lengthen. He leapt from his foaming horse and ran to the king with the disastrous message of the Prague revolt.

Processions had streamed to the Town Hall of the New Town in Prague to demand the release of those who had been imprisoned for their belief. A mighty column of believers in the sacrament in both kinds had been led by Jan Želivský with a monstrance in his hands. The New Town councillors had answered with a stone hurled from the Town Hall window. Upon which the people broke into the Town Hall and threw ten councillors from the windows. They had fallen on raised spears and swords and all of them had been killed.

The king listened to the messenger's report without a movement, and he felt the blood cease to run in his veins and the anger fill his heart and his head. He opened his mouth and cried out, but what words he meant to say could not be understood. All his anger and helplessness were in that cry, his bondage and fierce longing to rule. In that cry was the recognition that the time of his life was ending.

They carried him to his bed, struck down by apoplexy. He never entirely recovered. Thoughts and words died off within him and in the middle of August, when the woods and meadows round the New Castle called men to the hunt, he died, pierced by the arrow of death.

When the news was brought to the astrologer, he went to look at the St. Vitus cathedral. The spire was not yet demolished. Only a small part of it. The king had ended his life sooner, he had died before it was destroyed. So after all he died before it.

Žito the Magician

The Bohemian King Wenceslas IV. had a renowned magician at his court. He did many magical tricks for the king's amusement, and they were talked of all over Prague.

Once for instance the magician came before the king in ragged clothes, but these were immediately changed as he stood, no longer was he dressed as a beggar, but wore a costly court suit. But the courtiers were only beginning to be surprised when they saw how his magnificent garments disappeared and the magician stood there in a long cloak like a hermit.

He played innumerable pranks to entertain his king... During a banquet, for instance, he caused the king's jester's hands to turn magically into hoofs, and people at the table watched fascinated as the frightened wretch tried in vain to pick up his food.

The name of the magician was Žito.

Žito the magician did not accompany his king on horseback or in a carriage, as the other courtiers did, he drove in the procession with a three-in-hand of black cocks. That was how they drove through the streets of Prague, followed by astonished crowds, the king in a carriage drawn by six white horses, while the magician cracked his whip wildly over the heads of black cocks...

Once a Bavarian duke came to visit the Bohemian king. And in his train he brought two famous magicians.

And there was great competition at Prague Castle. The foreign magicians did their best not to be shamed before their duke.

But Žito the magician won gloriously - when the magicians looked out of the windows of Prague Castle he conjured antlers onto their heads - so big that they could not draw their heads

back into the feasting hall. Only when the courtiers had had their fill of laughing did Žito give in and conjure the antlers off their proud heads...

And when the German magicians did not want to admit their defeat, Žito the magician started to open his mouth to an immense width. The magicians realised what he intended - and fled. But Žito caught up with them - placed both the magicians in his mouth and swallowed them. He had a huge vat full of cold water brought and he spat them out into it.

Then it was said that no one had such a great magician as the Bohemian king.

He demonstrated the greatest magic.

But to be able to do it he had to sign over his soul to the devil.

So in the end his magical art availed him nothing - for all his sorcery he ended in hell.

Dalibor

n olden days there were some lords who were cruel to their bondsmen and others who used their power sensibly and with forethought. Bondsmen who had been subjected to harsh serfdom elsewhere fled to the estates of these latter. But no lord was allowed to keep another man's bondsman - it was regarded as stealing. Bondsmen were not allowed to choose their master, they were his property. If one escaped he was sent back to his former master in fetters. Or he escaped again, running further and further. How many bondsmen escaped from the estates of Adam of Ploskovice in Bohemia. And woe betide those he caught.

Sir Adam lived very well in the Ploskovice fortress, and he took no thought for the misery and suffering of his serfs. But the day came when all the suffering he had inflicted on them turned against him.

A mob armed with flails and axes advanced on the Ploskovice fortress. The bondsmen overcame the armed guards and searched the fortress. In vain did Sir Adam hide from them in the cellar. They found him and led him out into the courtyard. He stood terrified in the yard of his own fortress face to face with those to whom he had so recently given orders. Now the bondsmen gave the master orders.

Here is the contract according to which Sir Adam renounces his bondsmen and hands his fields and forests over to them. If he wishes to save his life, let him sign the contract. And how should Sir Adam not wish to save his life? With a trembling hand he signed.

And with the signed contract the representatives of the people of Ploskovice went to Sir Dalibor of Kozojedy. They requested him to take them on, for in those days bondsmen were not allowed to be without a master.

Dalibor of Kozojedy was known as a clement and just lord. He received the Ploskovice bondsmen kindly and took them on. He began to manage the Ploskovice estates, and for a time it seemed that peace and calm reigned in the region below the mountains of Central Bohemia.

But Adam of Ploskovice was preparing revenge against those who had taken his estates from him. And the greatest revenge he swore against Sir Dalibor of Kozojedy.

Sir Adam searched for a long time till he succeeded in finding and bribing a traitor. This man stole for him the contract Sir Adam had signed. As soon as Sir Adam had this contract in his hand he sued Dalibor of Kozojedy at the Prague court.

Dalibor of Kozojedy was apprehended and taken to the court in Prague Castle. At that time a new tower with a jail had just been built in the castle. A little cell in the new tower became Dalibor's home for many long months. The court was in no hurry to pass sentence on him.

Sir Adam had lords from the neighbouring estates and well-to-do friends in Litoměřice on his side. All of them were afraid lest their bondsmen might not rise against them too, so they supported Sir Adam's lawsuit fervently.

Dalibor had much time to think about his imprisonment and about freedom, but he could see no end in sight. The story is that in a dismal mood he paid his jailer to get a violin for him. He had never played the violin. Now he practised playing and the voice of the violin brought him comfort. The freedom that he had lost behind the mighty walls of the prison came back to him in song. Dalibor played the violin and sent his songs through the grated window of the tower out into the sun, high into the branches of the trees and to the clouds. The clouds bore the voice of his violin to his native region, to the people and places he loved.

Every evening a crowd of people gathered at the foot of the tower and listened to Dalibor playing. As he played so his listeners smiled or wiped their tears according to how he set his bow, whether sorrowfully or joyously. His songs told stories, wept or cheered so comprehensilly that everyone understood their language. The people fell in love with Dalibor's violin and they rewarded Dalibor in any way they could. They put food and drink into a basket and Dalibor hauled the basket up on a rope to the window of his cell.

Day by day the crowd beneath Dalibor's window grew, day by day grew Dalibor's fame. The judges began to be afraid of Dalibor of Kozojedy. Those crowds listening beneath the tower, where they not Dalibor's new friends? Did his violin not call for justice, his songs not hide the longing for fight and freedom? Was his violin not sowing a storm?

That violin had to be silenced, Dalibor had to be silenced. After months of his imprisonment the judges were in a hurry. They met and they condemned Dalibor to death. Death was to solve what the king and his queen did not know how to solve. The executioner beheaded Dalibor near to his tower.

In the evening the listeners gathered at the foot of the tower, but the violin was silent.

The legend of Dalibor, his violin and his death spread all over Prague and reached every corner of the Bohemian kingdom. The legend of a good master and his singing violin - of Dalibor, whom necessity taught to play the violin.

The tower was called after its prisoner - Daliborka.

The Church in Šárka

t is related that Prince Boleslav the Pious loved hunting and used to ride out on horseback to Šárka valley.

There one day a vast bear attacked him, and it looked as though the prince, who had not even time to draw his sword, would be torn to pieces by the wild beast.

But then there appeared beside him an old man with a shining face.

He raised his stick -

He touched the bear with it and at that moment the fierce creature was subdued and ran off into the forest...

The prince turned in amazement to the old man:

"I thank you for saving my life."

"Prince," said the old man, "it was not a bear that attacked you, it was an evil spirit that had taken on the likeness of a bear. It haunts this place because there are graves of murdered heathens here."

"Who lies buried here? asked the prince.

"Ctirad and his friends, who were killed in the Maidens' war."

The prince looked at the old man in surprise.

"Who are you, and how can you know of things that happened here so many years ago?"

The old man answered: "I know many things. I am one of the twelve apostles and my name is Matthew."

Then the old man turned into a shining cloud...

He disappeared.

The prince asked a servant who was hunting with him if he too had seen the old man he had been talking to.

"Yes," replied the servant, "but I could not see his face for the shining light."

When the prince returned to the castle after the hunt he told Bishop Adalbert - later sainted - about this meeting, and he advised the prince to have a church built at this place as a memorial to, and thanksgiving for, his miraculous salvation, and said that he should dedicate it to St. Matthew.

Prague Saint's Dedication Day

rague Saint's Dedication day has been celebrated since time immemorial.

This is the story told of its origin:

Prince Oldřich often used to go out hunting with his retinue. Once when they were chasing a stag, his precious cap got caught by a branch, and by the time he had set it on his head again, his retinue was lost in the forest.

The prince was alone and he wandered helplessly here and there about the woods.

In the end though he did come out from under the dark trees into a big clearing.

In the clearing there was a charcoal stack, so the prince thought there must be some charcoal-burner not far away.

He blew his horn.

A charcoal-burner came out of the wood and asked the prince what his wishes were.

When he heard that the prince wanted to find the way to Prague, the charcoal-burner thought a moment.

"Sir, I will gladly show you the way. But I see that you are tired. Wouldn't you like to visit my cottage and celebrate Dedication Day with us?"

It seemed an attractive offer to the exhausted prince.

He went to the charcoal-burner's home to celebrate with him, telling him that he was the prince's chamberlain and that his name was Mates.

He accepted all he was offered and in return invited the charcoal-burner to Prague.

"I'll be happy to come," agreed the charcoal-burner, "but you must roast a goose for me too."

The prince laughed and agreed he would.

Založení
pražského
Posvícení
M. Aleš
1904

On St. Martin's Day the charcoal-burner really did appear in Prague.

The prince had told the guard that if anybody were to ask for chamberlain Mates he was to be brought to him.

And so they took the poor charcoal-burner into the sovereign's magnificent hall. At the head of the hall sat - Mates. The charcoal-burner realised at once who it was who had been his guest.

He begged the prince to forgive him for not having shown him in the forest the respect due to a Bohemian prince.

But the prince only smiled and gave the charcoal-burner, as he had wished, a dish of goose.

When the charcoal-burner left the castle he was laden with so many gifts that he could hardly carry them.

And since that day the prince decreed that dedication day should be celebrated in Prague on St. Martin's Day - and the main meal on this ancient festival has to this day remained goose...

The Lamp

he legend about the golden lamp hanging over the grave of St. John of Nepomuk has been told in Prague for many generations.

One of the Prague goldsmiths grew poor - not that he was extravagant, so he could not blame himself, only fate. He had many children, and he wondered what would become of them when he could not feed them.

If I were to carry off the lamp hanging over the grave of St. John of Nepomuk, thought the goldsmith... I should be well off in a moment. I could make jewellery from the gold and sell it...

But -

But that would be stealing and that I cannot do.

Once, after a day full of worries, he fell asleep.

And St. John of Nepomuk appeared to him in a dream.

"Go to the church and take the golden lamp over my grave. I want to help you, go and fetch it. But do not forget me when you grow rich!"

The goldsmith wondered at the dream. But he did not dare to take the lamp.

The same dream came to him for three nights...

The goldsmith went to the St. Vitus Cathedral, and let himself be shut in there overnight, and he took down the lamp hanging over the saint's grave. In the morning, when the sacristan unlocked the cathedral and people started coming in, he went out of the church unobserved. At home he at once melted down the gold, so that no one could prove the theft.

He thought there would be a search for the lamp as soon as it was found to be missing.

But he heard no talk of any theft.

So he went to have a look in the St. Vitus Cathedral and

stood dumbfounded - a golden lamp still shone in its usual place, between the silver lamps.

He realised that a miracle had happened.

He grew rich, the gold from the lamp brought him luck.

And then he decided that it was high time for him to return the stolen lamp to the cathedral.

He made a wonderful lamp of pure gold.

And just when he had finished making it the gold lamp over the saint's grave really did disappear...

He took his own lamp and dedicated it to the cathedral. Thus it was it was that St. John, though in paradise, helped an unhappy Czech goldsmith.

Contents:

Eduard Petiška, Jan M. Dolan
Beautiful Stories of Golden Prague
Translated by Norah Hronková
Illustrations by Mikoláš Aleš
Lay-out by Karel Vilgus
Printed by G print, Ltd.
Published by Martin

If you liked these stories, there's another book for you.

Golem

For the first time, on the basis of precious, ancient sources, its author, Eduard Petiška, presents the old Prague Jewish legends and fairy tales in a modern way. The world of wise Prague Rabbis, the enigmatic Golem, the Prague Wandering Jew and many other fascinating figures, great and small, will open before you and bring Prague's ancient past nearer to you.

Would you like to know the magic world of Prague?

The book
A Guide to Mysterious Prague

is the first ever guide to the world of Prague ghosts, wraiths and phantoms - it can make your strolls through Prague's nooks and corners exciting. It also has a map on which you can find the haunts of Prague's weird ghosts...

Contact address for books on ancient Prague:

Baset
U Sanopzu 5
150 00 Praha 5
Czech Republic